Are You Ready? Choosing a Deeper Relationship with God

Anna Hill Moore

Copyright © 2016 by Anna Hill Moore

All rights reserved.

Book design by Anna Hill Moore.

No part of this book may be reproduced in any form or by any electronic or mechanical means including information storage and retrieval systems, without permission in writing from the author. The only exception is by a reviewer, who may quote short excerpts in a review.

Anna Hill Moore Books are available
for purchase through

Scripture verses are from the Holy Bible,
New International and King James versions

Anna Hill Moore
Visit my website at www.AnnaHillMoore.com

Printed in the United States of America
First Printing: April 2016
Published by Sojourn Publishing, LLC

ISBN: 978-1-62747-090-2
Ebook ISBN: 978-1-62747-091-9

Table of Contents

Introduction xi
Chapter 1. Ready? Or not ….. 1
Chapter 2. Finding Freedom in God's Love 5
Chapter 3. Freedom, Trust and Faith 7
Chapter 4. Choices 9
Chapter 5. Connection 15
Chapter 6. Relationship.. 17
Chapter 7. Speak, God … and help me hear............ 27
Chapter 8. Pride 31
Chapter 9. Living Life... 37
Chapter 10. Friendship.. 43
Chapter 11. Get Real.. 49
Chapter 12. Move Ahead 59
Chapter 13. Learn from the Best................................ 67
Chapter 14. Words 69
Chapter 15. Peace... 73
Chapter 16. Take a Closer Look 77
Chapter 17. Grow, and Be Healthy 81
Chapter 18. Set the Stage 85
Chapter 19. Boundaries, not Walls 89
Chapter 20. Priorities 93
Chapter 21. Prepare.. 97

Chapter 22. Seeking Support 99
Chapter 23. The Journey of a Lifetime 101
Epilogue 105

Dedication

This book is dedicated to my family and friends who have supported me every step along the way; to Dr. Stanley Young and his wife Becky, who were the instruments God used to introduce me to a deeper relationship with Him; but most of all to Jesus Christ, my Lord and Savior, my Sustainer, my Rock. May He be glorified through this book.

Forward

This book is an attempt to share with you what I have learned over the past few years as I have journeyed with God along my path in life. If I claimed it to be the "end all, be all, how to book," I would be deceiving you. Instead, I can honestly say that it is a meager offering from me to you, written with the hope that it may provoke you to consider where you are and where you want to be in your walk with God. It is an easy read. It is an encouraging read. It is not meant to condemn or to cause guilt or shame. It is designed to help you think, to simplify, to perceive God's amazing love toward you and His desire for relationship with you. If you are longing for more, if you have a hunger in your soul that you cannot understand, perhaps this little book will help you. I pray you would be blessed and encouraged as you read it. Understand that God desires communion with you individually, and that He is there, ever present, patient beyond our human capacity and understanding. He longs for your companionship. He longs to be active in your life. He loves you beyond measure. If you seek Him, you will find Him.

> *But if from there you seek the Lord your God, you will find him if you seek him with all your heart and with all your soul. Deuteronomy 4:29 NIV*

Acknowledgements

Without the support of my husband, I would never have been able to write this book. For this I am eternally grateful. My children have been supportive as well, especially when mom took time to sequester herself for writing! My love runs deeply for my family.

My dear friend Linda Brooks has been a never ending encourager... She has the gift of encouragement. Just ask her husband. She has believed in me and in my effort to be obedient to what God has asked me to do. I trust the Lord will greatly reward her for using her spiritual gift. Thank you, my friend! I am so blessed to have you in my life.

My friend Mary Wightman has provided encouragement and exhortation, spurring me to follow God's promptings in my life while not sparing me from His truths. She makes me think and reminds me that God's timing is best.

Thank you, Mary. I remember when God introduced us and am forever grateful to Him for your friendship.

My prayer partners in our Monday Morning Connection Bible Study group have been a source of comfort and support, and again I express my gratitude to these ladies and to our Lord.

I would be remiss to not include all those friends and family members who have encouraged me along the way, who have prodded me to follow the Lord's path, who have helped me think and grow and explore. These are too numerous to name, but you know who you are. I love you, and I appreciate your pouring into my life.

Finally, I would like to offer sincere appreciation and thanks to Tom Bird, Gwen Payne, Ramajon Cogen, and all those at Sojourn Publishing for making this book possible, and the process so rewarding! Thanks so much, you guys! It has been a pleasure working with you! I could not have done this without your guidance and encouragement.

Introduction

Life is a journey. Sometimes it seems long. At other times, it seems brief. Nevertheless, it is a journey which we all must take, and each of us wants our life to be the best it can be. Life is only made better and sweeter as we draw closer to God. I invite you to make your walk better by deepening your relationship with Him.

Join me in this adventure we call life. Take time to consider the words ahead, words from my heart to yours, and see if you find a path to freedom in Him, a path to fulfillment, a path to peace. Allow Him to speak to you as He walks beside you on your own journey home. Rest in Him. He will be your Sustainer.

Chapter 1:
Ready? Or not …

Are you ready? Are you ready for a change? Are you ready for a deeper walk? Are you ready to surrender all? Are you ready to look beyond today and your small little world and take the next step with God? Maybe you are. Maybe you aren't. Maybe time and time again you've tried and you've fallen back. But what about now? Where are you *now*?

Two years ago, I took that step. I moved ahead. I was ready. It was His time. He gave me what I asked for because I meant it… Deep inside my heart, I was ready to surrender myself. In that surrender, I found new freedom. It was a freedom I hadn't known before. It was freedom and an inner peace, even in the midst of my chaos. That's not to say life has been easy. By far, I would say this has been one of the most difficult times I have faced. I was emotionally distraught and sometimes destitute. He helped me, and is helping me, through the storms by providing me that daily quiet time when I am alone with Him.

No time, you say? I found time. Rather He found time for me... Not a morning person by any means, He has allowed me to awaken more easily, and my desire has been to be with Him, to spend time talking with and listening to Him. Through those times, He has given me promise, strength, comfort, insight, and clarity. He has taught me to walk in obedience, a task at which I do not always excel. He has taught me not to be concerned about what others think of what I do or don't do—just to follow His promptings. As long as I listen to Him and use the principles I read in the scripture, I live life without regret.

Notice I didn't say without difficulty, conflict or pain. I said without regret. This trumps them all. This walk is not about living selfishly. It is about living ***selflessly***. We are called to service, to ministry, to growth. We are called to think as individuals, not to move as a herd. My decisions must be based on His direction, not on my circumstances. He has called me to obey.

If you are His child, He has called you to obey also. Not to just exist. Not to just get through the day. To obey so you can make a difference in your world.

Obey. We don't like that word. It makes us think of the three R's: rules, regulations and restrictions. That is not what I am referring to when I emphasize the word obey. I am talking about following God's prompting and direction for your life, moment by moment, day by day. He offers you a lifetime of love, and it is yours for the taking. A free gift. Without strings attached.

He doesn't want slaves. He doesn't want hired help. He wants children. He wants children who love Him, who honor Him, and who listen to Him. He wants to spend time with His children. He wants to speak to His children. He loves them. He loves all people, so much that he sacrificed His one and only son, sentencing Him to die a cruel death on a cross, just so you and I can have the privilege of being called His.

Anna Hill Moore

Blessed are those who have learned to acclaim you, who walk in the light of your presence, Lord.
Psalm 89:15 NIV

Chapter 2:
Finding Freedom in God's Love

Are you ready? Ready to be loved unconditionally? Well, here's your chance. No, let me rephrase that. Here's your calling.

You are called to be His so that He can lavish you with His love. You are loved. Be His. Surrender to freedom. Freedom from unmet demands, conditional love, and performance standards. Just be free. "You will find that freedom in Me," He says to you. "I created the world. I created you to be in the world. I love you. I want you to experience my love. It's a love like no other." You can't buy it. You can't order it off QVC. You can't return it. It just is…

God's love knows no bounds of any kind. He loves through time, through space, through circumstances. He loves everyone. His love is eternal, unmatchable. His love is deeper than any love you will feel for another person. Think how deeply you love your child (children). His love is infinitely deeper, and He wants to give it to you. He wants to share life with you, to walk your path with you. He wants to be your everything.

He has a plan for your life. His plan is best. He knows your path. He knows where you will stumble. He knows when you will leave the path, and He knows exactly when you will get back on it. Trust Him—with yourself, your life, your loved ones. Trust Him and let Him show Himself to you. Jesus Christ stays the same. God is trustworthy. Jesus' death and resurrection proved it.

> *As the Father has loved me, so have I loved you. Now remain in my love.*
> *John 15:9 NIV*

Chapter 3:
Freedom, Trust and Faith

Are you ready? Ready to be free? Our freedom in America came at a high price. It is maintained at a high price. Our spiritual freedom cost Jesus his life, and cost God his son. But it was a price that had to be paid only once. That's all it took. We don't have to worry about losing that freedom once we accept it. No one can take it away. Nothing anyone can do would ever take it away. God will not ask for it back.

Freedom comes through trust, and trust is an act of faith. Even weak faith can trust. As we trust God, He demonstrates His faithfulness to us, and our faith grows. Maybe that is why it may seem that older Christians have more faith. They have lived longer and have had more time and experience trusting God.

That doesn't mean you have to wait to have faith and trust. Trust is a choice you make moment by moment. As you trust Him for the little things in life, and acknowledge that these are by His hand alone, you will begin to see Him revealed in the moments. As you become more aware of His work in your life, He will reveal more of Himself to you.

Have an open spirit to the Lord. Try not to let the daily activities of life distract you. If you cannot see Him at work, talk to Him about it. Tell Him your worries and concerns. Then listen, and watch. As you ask and look for His hand, you will see it.

So if the Son sets you free, you will be free indeed.
John 8:36 NIV

Chapter 4:
Choices

I don't believe in coincidences. It's a nice word, but in my world, everything happens for a reason. When my world begins to fall apart, and I have no clue why, I know there is a reason. I may never know the reason, but that doesn't change the fact that there is one.

Some things happen as a consequence of our choices. Some things happen like a domino effect because of the choices made by another. Some things happen because of our pride or selfishness.

I cannot begin to explain the "why" of many circumstances. Yet we as humans always look for a reason. We don't seem to be satisfied without one. We in our humanness cannot comprehend why bad things happen. I cannot explain it, but I believe it is because we live in a fallen and broken world.

I do not believe that God causes bad things to happen to us, but I do believe that He is fully aware that they will happen. He knows the outcome. He knows how it will affect us. But he is not the mean jailer just waiting for us to do something so he can punish us for His own pleasure.

God loves us and wants the best for us. He knows what is going to happen to us and the choices we will make. Yet He *still* loves us and longs to bless us. He hurts when we hurt. He sings over us just as we would sing over a newborn. (Zephaniah 3:17) And how much we love our babies!

So are you ready? What is the next step? Do we end it here and walk away, or do we forge ahead, one step at a time? Or maybe two steps forward and one step back… The next step is the decision. Once you make the decision, you will know what to do.

Will you decide to take him up on His offer? Will you trust Him and find freedom? Or will you stay enslaved to your current spiritual life? Are you a prisoner? Or are you free? Are you locked in a cage or running a mouse maze of religion? Or are you in the free state of relationship with the One True Living God? You are either captive or free. Decide which you are. Choose what you will choose—to stay the same, or to change and grow. Weigh the consequences. Staying the same means seeing same results. Doing something different yields different results. This is not a radical thought! You know it to be true …

If you choose to change, what then? There is much fear associated with change. The known is often more palatable than the unknown. If you change, what would your friends and family think? How would they react? Would it change your relationship with your spouse/significant other?

If your spouse/significant other is not a believer, it will definitely change your relationship. Hopefully it will be for the better as you become a more Christ-like individual. Maybe you will have more grace for your partner. Maybe you will be more peaceful and more pleasant. Whatever the change, continue to honor your spouse and your marriage. God will surely bless this effort.

But what are we really talking about here? We are talking about change for the good. How could knowing and doing God's will be worse for you than staying the same? Well, sometimes there are significant consequences to change that affect us. For example, if your spouse is an unbeliever, or a Christian who is not really interested in growing, your enthusiasm for spiritual development may disrupt the harmony you think you have in your relationship. Your spouse may think he is being displaced by God. It may be hard to see how we can love God first and love our spouse as we should. I have fought with this thought myself and have struggled to reconcile it. I am not sure I have a good answer, except that God ordained marriages and He has an interest in their health. All that being said, just because you are on a mission to improve your relationship with God, don't expect your spouse to jump on board, or your boyfriend/girlfriend to understand. As with any experience, if they have not been there themselves, they cannot fully understand.

Shared experiences create deep spiritual bonds. Choose wisely with whom you will share your experiences. Those people become connected to you for the long haul.

Sometimes we cannot choose with whom we share experiences, but we can choose the level of intimacy with each person in our lives. Only those trustworthy individuals who are like minded should be allowed at your core. Like layers of an onion, we have a variety of people in our lives. Not all can be at the heart level…

Above all else, guard you heart, for everything you do flows from it.
Proverbs 4:23 NIV

Chapter 5:
Connection

People come into our lives for a reason. Some are with us for just a moment, some for days, weeks, months, years or even for a lifetime. But when our paths cross, God has put them there. Search for the reason. Search for the connection. We are created for connection, for fellowship. Solitary life is not the ideal.

Perhaps some of us cannot enjoy deeper connection, maybe because of fear. Maybe it is because our self-worth is compromised. Maybe we just don't want to put the effort into maintaining a healthy relationship. Maybe it's because it hasn't been modeled for us. Whatever the reason, it is a choice. It is our choice how we relate to others.

Sharing the journey of life with someone, even for brief periods, is a privilege for us. We are blessed when we walk with someone else on their journey. Even as we try to bless others, we often come away with the blessing. Shared lives means shared joy, shared hurts, shared griefs. The Apostle Paul tells us to bear one another's burdens, thereby fulfilling the law of Christ (Galatians 6:3). That does not mean to do all the work for someone, but it means that we are to help them, to be there for them, to support them as we can.

What about people who are toxic to you? People whose situation in life seems to absolutely suck the life out of you? One must proceed with caution in these relationships because they can damage you at your core. First and foremost, you must focus on your spiritual health and your relationship with God. If you do this, the rest of it will fall into place. No, that doesn't mean that life is rosy and cheery all the time. It means that you can trust His guidance, His prompting and His activity in your life. Remember, He loves you unconditionally. Accepting this love is your choice.

But if we walk in the light, as He is in the light, we have fellowship with one another.
1 John 1:7a NIV

Chapter 6:
Relationship

Who is God and why should you care? The creator of the universe, the one who put the stars in place, who designed the natural laws, He is God. He is worthy of our praise and adoration. He didn't just set the world in motion and abandon it. He continues to create and be at work in daily life.

King David asked, "Who is man that thou art mindful of him?" (Psalm 8:4) He spent time with God in his daily life, oftentimes alone in the field. Quiet, alone, just the sheep for company, David had only God to talk to. Seems there wasn't much to distract in that day without television, telephones, and internet. It was just survival. Day to day life.

How many times God had delivered David! He knew God because he spent time with Him. He was a man after God's own heart. When did

David stumble? He stumbled when he moved away from God. We do not know all the details of his life, but I doubt he had an extended time alone with God after he became King David. Maybe we can learn from his example and try to keep time with God a priority, regardless of how busy our lives become.

I remember a time in my life when I could hear God's voice clearly. I saw Him at work in my life in the little things. I lost that for a while as my life became hectic, and it seemed I had no time. When daily cares and difficult relationships took their toll, I cried out to God—but I found myself moving away from Him. Over the past few years, I am more aware. I again see Him at work in my life and in the lives of those around me. I acknowledge His presence in my daily life. He has given me a freedom I had not known before.

Life is a work in progress, a sequence of events that build on each other. I can look back over my life and see His handprint–times when I have struggled and times when I have felt triumphant. I see the path I have been on, but I cannot see the path ahead. My map doesn't give me my ultimate destination, but it gives me signposts, leading me onward.

My map is my Bible which tells me how I am to live. It is not hard to understand. The core teaching is to love God and to love others as you love yourself. We have self-love. It sometimes becomes self-loathing. We may stumble, fall, make huge mistakes, and live a life that we never wanted to live. It is in those times that we are prone to self-loathing.

Self-loathing may occur when our reality does not meet our dreams or expectations of life, situations or relationships. It may happen as a result of other's condemnation or abuse of us. Self-loathing is our anger turned inward towards our self. We may feel useless, tainted, less than what we want to be. We may feel helpless and despise that about ourselves. We may feel powerless to change.

Satan takes this opportunity of our self-loathing to hurt us, to beat us down, or to just make us unconcerned. We have to recognize that while God's voice may be convicting, it will not be condemning. "There is therefore now no condemnation to those who are in Christ" (Romans 8:1).

Does that mean that we can do whatever we want and not care? Absolutely not, but it means that we will not be condemned by Him. He loves us. He looks at us and says, "My precious child, I love you. I only wish you knew how much…"

Maybe our spiritual growth parallels what we see in our children. We meet God, and we love Him like a small child loves his parents. Then, as we are in the relationship longer, it becomes humdrum, casual, taken for granted. We have some interaction but we become more independent of Him.

Then comes defiance (ergo, middle school age). Defiance leads to rebellion (teens and early 20s) which will hopefully resolve into a more caring, loving and adult relationship with God.

I am mainly sharing what I have seen in my life, and in no way to I claim this to be a universal experience. As I age, I grow in Him. I see some Christians grow away from Him as they age, and I wonder why. Maybe life has been hard, and they are tired. Or maybe, like David they gave up their time with and focus on Him. Or still yet, maybe they had neither.

Maybe they were going through the motions, obeying rules instead of developing a relationship with Him. Whatever the reason, it saddens me to see it. I pray I do not become such a person. I want to maintain my relationship with God, and I want it to grow deeper with time.

So where does that leave me? It leaves me with a need for action. I have already made the decision, by stating this is what I want. How do I go about doing this? How can I maintain?

I must be disciplined. That is an ugly word for me because I prefer spontaneity and what I perceive as the freedom it brings me. However, I have learned that routines can be freeing. That sounds paradoxical but it is true. Routines free your mind from thinking too much and worrying about what you need to do or have not done. A routine at home frees you in that way. A routine with God frees you even more. It refreshes your spirit. It gives you some thing to hold onto, something to look forward to, on those hard days.

What discipline do I need? I need daily time alone with Him for starters. That is hard, especially with a busy, active family. The urgent trumps the important in many instances. Things demand my time and attention. Laundry, for example, is a never-ending battle. I do the laundry at my house, and my family always needs clean clothes. Meals are a challenge with differing schedules and after school activities. So these things are "in my face," so to speak. Many may comment that I should be better organized. No doubt I should be, but that would not fix the situation. My life is still busy, and so is yours.

Thus I have embarked on an effort to simplify my life in many areas. I long to control my environment and to manage the chaos in my house. At least, I perceive it as chaos. I am a work in progress although I have made great strides in the last few years.

My constant goal is to simplify—lifestyle, environment, routines. I want to teach my child to live simply. The demands of a simple life enable more spiritual freedom. The Lord began speaking to me about this several years ago. My spirit resonated with this idea. I try. Some days, weeks, months, or years, I am better at it than others.

When I am in my routine, I do better. When I allow my routine to slip, I fall behind and I begin to feel that my mind and spirit are cluttered. My soul is then no longer in a positive place. More importantly, my relationship to God takes a back seat. He gets pushed aside. Oh, I continue to talk to Him, just not deeply. And I find that I don't listen very well when this happens. I don't attend to His voice.

I am so much more peaceful when I do take that time with Him. I find myself more at ease, more self-assured, and more confident when I have spent time with Him. That is probably because I am walking in His power and not my own.

So how do I keep the momentum going with God? I make the choice. I make the decision. I take action.

I recall the year my youngest daughter started middle school. I have been through this once, and I remember how difficult it was. I dreaded the coming years, but I was determined that I would persevere! As school was about to begin, I knew that I wanted our mornings to go smoothly. I did not want morning chaos to color my day or my daughter's day, so I talked to God about it. I asked Him for help.

I wanted to start my day with a quiet time. I am not a morning person. I never have been. I asked God to help me be a morning person, but that never happened. What has happened is that I now get up an hour or so before my daughter, read my devotional and scripture, journal, and pray.

What a difference it makes! Oh my goodness. Now I absolutely long to get up and be with Him. Well, maybe not every single day…but I long to be in His presence, to be in communion with Him. One hour does not seem like enough time now. I want more. I am at peace when I am spending time with Him. When I am struggling or not at peace, I can talk it over with Him. But now I want more! I miss it so much if something happens and I cannot have that time.

I have on occasion been plain lazy—but not very often. I love my time with Him. And it is not a legalistic checklist quiet time because somebody told me I should do it. It is a desire from my heart. Therein lies the difference.

How did this happen? I have been talking about needing to do this for years, wanting to do it. Notice I said talking about wanting to do it. I did sort of want it, but not at the deepest level of my heart. I guess the bottom line is that this time, I was ready.

How did I get ready? I cannot tell you exactly. I just know that I was. I was surrendered in my heart. There was a release of self and a request for His presence. God is faithful, even when we are not.

People have tried to guilt us into a quiet time with words like "You told God that you would be there. He showed up and you didn't." That does not help me at all. It just makes me feel like a failure. It does not motivate me. Guilting someone in to something does not work for long, because that person begins to resent it.

What changed in my equation? What changed for me was *me*. I moved aside. But even as I moved aside, my desire for His presence was selfish. My motives were about me: about making my mornings better, my child's experience better, my life better.

But as I began to meet with Him and experience Him on a daily basis, I found my motivation was more about the relationship, about being with Him, and about hearing from Him. What began as a selfish desire to make my life easier, blossomed into a sweet, spirit-led urgency in my heart and mind to spend time with the Lord I love.

> *I love those who love me, and those who seek me find me.*
> *Proverbs 8:17 NIV*
>
> *My heart says of you, "Seek His face!" Your face, Lord, will I seek.*
> *Psalm 27:8 NIV*

Chapter 7:
Speak, God ... and help me hear

I have had some amazing experiences in my quiet time, and I have had some so-so experiences. Regardless, God uses each and every one. Sometimes a thought from my quiet time will wander around in my head all day. Sometimes, I am so enthused by what I read, heard, or am thinking that I am absolutely bursting to share it with others. Sometimes I come to work so happy that people look at me funny. Try spending an hour with the Lord and see how it affects you.

Pastor Scott Cagle of Northstar Church in Knoxville said something in one of his sermons that has stayed with me. He said if the King of the universe takes time to say something to you, the least you can do is write it down. I decided to do that. I began to read a book on prayer and to journal what God was saying to me. During this time, God gave me a promise, and I am looking forward to when He completes it as He said He would. You see, I trust Him. I find that He is faithful to His word.

God speaks to each of us in different ways. The primary source is from the scripture. I am fascinated when I read a scripture passage that I have read several times before and I see something new. Or I see it in a different light. We can apply the principles we read in scripture to our lives and know that, by doing so, we are following His will.

But more satisfying to me is when I hear that still, small voice, and I recognize it as His. If I follow His prompting, I do not have bad results. If I do not heed when He warns me, I have bad results. I remember when God spoke to me clearly about an issue in my life. I did not heed the warning, and I saw come to fruition what He had indicated would happen. I wish I had listened.

But we cannot change the past. We can only learn from it. I hope I learned. The future will show whether I did learn. Lives can be affected when we do not listen to Him.

Blessed are those who listen to me, watching daily at my doors, waiting at my doorway.

Proverbs 8:34 NIV

Chapter 8:
Pride

What if my will gets in the way of what He wants? How do I move myself aside?

What is it about my will anyway?

I have come to the conclusion that my will is related strictly to my pride. My pride takes over and lets me think that I know better than God, that I have the right answers.

Pride is subtle. It sneaks in when we are not looking. People say "pride goes before a fall" and they generally say "the Bible says…" somewhere around it. That's not what the Bible says. The Bible says that pride goes before destruction (Proverbs 16:18). Destruction is very different from a fall. With a fall, you can get up, clean up, patch up, heal up, and move on. Destruction is just that: completely destroyed. If you can even recover from destruction, think how long it would take to put the pieces back together.

What do you think of when you hear the word "destruction?" I think of the Twin Towers at the World Trade Center. They are gone. Absoutely gone. Lives were lost. The rebuilding process is long, and it will never be the same. In some ways it will be better with a different support structure and newer security measures, but the new buildings will always be in the shadow of that day in history when the Towers crumbled, so many lives were lost, and our culture was changed. Likewise, our lives can be rebuilt. The process is long and hard, but we will always live in the shadow of our past.

So pride scares me. I do not want destruction in my life.

If we want to avoid personal destruction, we need to be aware of that insidious pride that sneaks in unawares. Being prideful is different from taking pride in something. I take pride in my children, but I do not want to have a pride that hinders me from being what and who I should be. If my child were in trouble and needed help, I would not want to have so much pride that I would not listen to others when they voiced concerns about her. Maybe that is not the best example, but perhaps you can relate to it. The bottom line is: pride can be destructive.

My pride is not necessarily visible to those around me. It is not necessarily visible to me. I have to be on constant guard and ask God to point out areas of pride in my life. He has the clear vision. Mine is tainted by wanting to preserve my self picture/self esteem. We, at our core, want to protect ourselves. Let's try to look at ourselves through God's eyes, to see ourselves as He sees us. We will not get a complete picture, because we do not have the full knowledge and understanding that He has. After all, He is God.

How does He see us? Oh, my friend! We are so very precious to Him! He loves us with and everlasting love and underneath are the everlasting arms (Deuteronomy 33:27), just as Elizabeth Elliott has reminded so many over the years on her radio broadcast. We are so precious to Him that He gave His son as a sacrifice for our sin. His only son...

Could you do that with your child? I have asked myself that question, and just do not think I could do that... Give up my daughter(s)? Even to save the world? I don't think I have that in me. I am glad I am not God.

Yet He may ask me to sacrifice my child in a different way. When I think of that, I recognize that my children are not mine. They are on loan from God. They are His children. His will should be done in their lives. My job is to raise them to know Him, to give them every opportunity to be all they can be in His purpose. They can rely on Him, but ultimately it is their choice, just as it is your choice.

Jesus didn't come to die and to be resurrected just to give us a pass to heaven, although that is terrific and I look forward to it. He came to bring us into a right relationship with God our creator so that we may have ***abundant*** life. Our ultimate purpose is to let His light shine through us so that others may see Him and have the opportunity to be in relationship with Him. We find it hard to move over and allow that to happen. How do we do it? We live life in Him day to day.

When pride comes, then comes disgrace, but with humility comes wisdom.
Proverbs 11:2 NIV

Pride goes before destruction, a haughty spirit before a fall.

Proverbs 16:18 NIV

Chapter 9:
Living Life

Living life day to day is our only option. We only have this moment. We are not guaranteed tomorrow. We cannot live in the past. We should plan for the future, but we need to live in the now. We need to be fully present and make the most of each day that God gives us. We are instructed by Jesus in the book of John to abide in Him, and He promises abundant life when we do.

Abundant life does not equate to material possessions, although most of us would not complain about material possessions. Abundant life happens when we find that joy in everyday living, everyday occurrences, and our relationships.

When God brings new people in to my life who touch me in some way, that is abundant living. Where would our journey be without them? Dull, blank, boring, meaningless to me… Just living life to get by is not abundant living.

Christ calls us to follow Him, to tell others as we go, to love our neighbors as ourselves, to be the beacon on the hill. In essence, He calls us to make a difference in the lives of others. How you make a difference depends on the person. For some people, it is a tangible act like making food for them when they are sick. For some, it is as simple as a smile that can brighten their day.

Once I did an experiment. First, let me explain that I am not one whose face is automatically set in a smile. There are some people you know who always have a smile on their face. When I am not smiling, my daughter tells me I look mean. My husband would be kinder and just label me as looking severe. He knows me and has come to understand that just because my face looks like that, it does not mean that I really am severe.

So my experiment went like this. One day, I made a conscious effort to smile all day long and at everyone I met. I also looked at them directly. The most amazing things happened. 1) I felt happy. 2) They invariably smiled back.

Some even spoke and shared a pleasantry with me. It was an eye opening experience for me. Now I try to smile more because it occurred to me that I may be the only one who shares a smile with that person for the entire day. As we go, we need to be like Him.

Another way to be like Jesus as we go is to recognize when people are hurting. The world is full of hurting people—deeply hurting people. Jesus was there for them. He, being God, knew what was going on in their lives. We, not being God, cannot know those things. But we can try to be more alert to the pain others are feeling. We don't need to make it our own pain, to take ownership of it, but we need to be able to sympathize and genuinely care.

Notice the word genuinely…not just meaningless words or good intentions, but true caring. That does not imply that you have to necessarily do anything or try to fix whatever the situation for them. But it does mean you can allow them to talk or offer to pray with or for someone. Maybe they do not have anyone in their life who prays for them or who cares. You never know another person's situation. If God prompts you to pray or to do, follow His prompting.

The Bible tells us that we are to comfort as we have been comforted (2 Corinthians 1:4). When we have experienced what another is experiencing, we can move beyond sympathy to empathy.

Empathy is experiencing those feelings with that person. Just as someone without the desire you have to grow spiritually cannot understand your desire for it, neither can we understand others' plights unless we have walked a similar path.

We should bear in mind that even if the path is similar, no two paths are exactly alike. So when you empathize with someone, don't think you know everything about their problem/situation. Be sympathetic/empathetic, but not a know-it-all. People have to work through their situations themselves, process the issue at their own pace. Sometimes they just need an understanding ear. Sometimes they just need a hug and to hear someone say, "I am so sorry you are going through all of this." Comfort others with the comfort you have received, and point them to the Father of comfort (2 Corinthians 1:3-4).

Above all, continue to abide in Christ and reap the rewards of a close relationship with Him. The spiritual fruit you bear will be a natural consequence of that intimacy with Him.

I have come that they may have life, and have it to the full.
John 10:10b NIV

Chapter 10:
Friendship

Impacting the lives of others is what we are here for. We make a difference in ways we may not anticipate. Connection is so important for the health of our souls. And it seems the world is very disconnected. Many people, few real connections...

I have had days and weeks when I have felt somewhat isolated and alone. Maybe you have experienced it. What I discovered is that there are people just like me who feel disconnected.

How do we resolve that dilemma? The first thing is to be connected with God. The second thing is to find people of like faith, core values, and beliefs who can understand and support you in your efforts. Often we are in similar circumstances and just don't know it.

When I say find someone, it's not like I mean go to E-harmony and advertise. ☺ I mean for you to ask God to place the people you need in your life. He will do it. Be open to it. It may happen when you least expect it.

Here is my example. I met one of my very best friends at a party. It was a party I did not want to attend, but felt I needed to because it was a work party. It was at someone's home with a rather large group of folks. I began a conversation with this woman who I had not met before. I had just finished the Experiencing God course at my church (within the previous year), and I was very open to Him putting people in my path. This lady and I talked. I cannot tell you what it was about because I cannot remember. But it was enough to know that she was having some struggles.

Details evade me, but the long and short of it is that later that week, I took her a Homelife magazine that I thought might help her with her struggles. The friendship blossomed from there. She became closer to the Lord as she found her deeper need for Him in her life.

She and I remain close friends although we rarely see each other. We occasionally speak on the phone. We contact each other with prayer needs. We share the wonderful things God is doing in our lives. She is a true friend whom I cherish. God has so blessed me through her presence in my life. I cannot thank Him enough. We each have our struggles but we know we can count on the other to lift us up in prayer and to be faithful to remember us before the Lord. When you connect with someone like she and I have connected, it is an amazingly special relationship.

How wonderful to have God-ordained friends in our lives! I cannot tell you how much it has meant to me, especially as I am growing older and my children are growing up. I have a stamp that I need to use that says "One good friend is better than 10 bad ones." It is so true. ONE good friend can make a world of difference in your life.

I have a core group of women who are my prayer buddies and Bible study companions. God has blessed me through them in ways you could not believe. It is so good to have friends who know you well, know your weaknesses and your struggles, and still love you.

Remember, God created us for fellowship. We are part of the church universal, and our Christian family is of great value to us. If you do not have such a friend, ask God to help you participate in a Bible study or women's group to give yourself an opportunity to be surrounded by like-minded women. To have a friend, you have to be one.

If you have been hurt in friendship before, you may be reluctant to connect. Give yourself an opportunity. Ask God for guidance. Seek wise counselors. Maybe you desire a mentoring relationship. Ask God. Trust Him. He wants the best for you. He loves you.

Be involved, but don't be so involved that you miss out on what is most important. We can fill our time with busyness to escape the pain and difficulties in our lives. This just lets them grow deeper roots.

As I grew up, I was very busy in church. I thought that was what being a true Christian was all about. If you weren't there every time the door was open, you were a heathen! As a young married woman, I continued in that habit that I had learned with the mindset of attendance and busyness equating to spirituality and spiritual health.

Don't get me wrong... We need to attend church. We need to be active. But we need to be led by the Holy Spirit in our activities and not be guilted into something that is not meant for us to do. People mean well, but often they are looking to fill a need. If you are available, it may not be about your ability or calling but about your availability.

I think this is a dangerous thing, and where we have so often gone wrong at church. Just because I am present, it doesn't mean that I am the right person for that job.

No. This is a word we need to learn to utilize. But instead of just saying no to everything, if we are in a good steady relationship with our Heavenly Father, we will know what we should do. We will not have to wonder whether or not we should do something.

Beware, though. Most folks do not like to hear the word no. They also don't like to hear the phrase, "Let me pray about it." I find it funny that Christians scoff at that phrase. We *should* pray about things.

But there are some things we do not need to pray about. I know beyond a shadow of a doubt that I do not need to be on a budget and finance committee. It is not my talent. It is not my gift. God wants me to use the gifts that he has given me.

That does not meant that He does not want me to learn and grow, but it means that He wants me to be me—the me that he created me to be. This is our freedom in Christ: to be who He made us!

Blessed be the name of the Lord! He made me. He made you.

He knows what He wants us to do. All we have to do is be faithful. He is faithful, even when we are not.

So what is it God that wants you to do? Simply put, He wants you to be the best you that you can be. We continue to grow and develop throughout life. If we stop, we die—maybe not physically, but inside. We are meant to thrive, not just survive. We thrive in His presence. Therefore, we should diligently seek His presence.

You will seek me and find me when you seek me with all your heart.
Jeremiah 29:13 NIV

Chapter 11:
Get Real

Have you been around people who absolutely bring out the best in you? That is what God does. That is what He wants for you…if you want it, too. He will not force it. You can be the best *you* through His guidance and direction.

Think about it. I have found that I am a better person, a happier person, a more fulfilled person, a more pleasant person to be around when I allow Him to direct me. I resisted for many years, claiming an independence and self-reliance which I finally identified as simple pride. It still sneaks in occasionally. If someone congratulates me on a job well done, or compliments me, I have to fight the pride. It just sneaks in as a part of my human nature. I want His divine nature in me.

Sometimes I feel like a dual personality with my human nature and God's divine nature now part of me. Paul would call me a carnal Christian when I am ruled by my humanity. It is a constant struggle because of what we are: human.

My most frustrating thing is being human. My frailties and faults are frustrating. I mostly do not like it when I mess up, and then I say I do not like being human. But if I examine the true issue, I would say it boils down to pride, and the perfectionism is an outlet of the pride.

Most of my issues, and maybe most people's issues, are related directly to pride. The only way to manage our pride is to be in constant contact with the Father, to seek His will and His agenda in our lives. But for that to happen, we have to agree that He is God and that He deserves our best, our focus.

How do we do this on a daily basis? We must have that time set aside. If it is important to us we will get it done, isn't that what the experts say? So how does it become important? Look at your life, your schedule. Think about how you spend your time. Thirty minutes of a sitcom could translate to thirty minutes with God, but it requires some sacrifice on your part.

It means you have to look at your life and prioritize, decide what is important, not just for the now but for the long haul. And while eternity is the ultimate long term issue, you have much life ahead of you. None of us want less life than we could have. All of us want the best. If making a daily commitment of your time and your attention could make such a difference for you, isn't it worth the investment?

But it is your choice—your decision. Don't be guilted into it because that motivation will not last. You will resent God and whoever suggested it.

If you want to think about what you will get out of this time with Him, you can look in the scripture: peace, not like this world gives; love; comfort; acceptance; wisdom is yours for the asking. I could give you all kinds of reasons to do this, but it has to be yours. You have to own it.

Try not to be afraid of God. He is not waiting to destroy you. He is not waiting to have you do something you hate doing.

When I was a little girl, I was afraid to surrender to Him because I was worried that He would send me to Africa to be a missionary. I would have to leave my family. I did not want to do that.

What I learned was that God gives us desires in our hearts and these are the desires he matches with His calling. If I had longed to be a missionary, He would have called me to that. I lived in fear for a long time… unnecessarily.

It was really after I surrendered to Him that I realized that He did not want me to be a career missionary in Africa. He had something else in mind for me. Where my future lies, I do not know. He is moving in my life and change is in the air, so to speak. It is interesting to contemplate. Even though I do not know what is ahead, I know that He has my very best interest at heart, and that He will take care of me.

My best times have been when I was totally surrendered to Him and knew that I was living in complete obedience to His will. I was where I needed to be, doing what I needed to be doing, and responding to His promptings. I was alert to and aware of His movement in my daily life.

Through that time, I saw Him use me to touch lives. What a blessing and joy it is to know that you are in His will! It was as close to euphoria as I have ever come.

Occasionally God will give me the words for poetry. I have shared a few verses in the past with my friends who also know my heart. They in turn have been blessed. But not through me. It is through my allowing God to use me. He can work through us to bless others. We need to let His light and His love shine. We may be the only way others will experience Him or be introduced to Him.

I have come to realize that I can do nothing without Him. I cannot take a breath, think a thought, write a word, move, or see. Nothing can I do without Him. Every breath, every heartbeat is a gift from God. I recognize it and I praise Him for it. I testify to this today to give Him glory for anything I accomplish. It is all of Him. I can do nothing in and of myself. It is His strength.

Some have argued that it is my intelligence, my brain, or my creativeness. But I am here to say: I am nothing apart from Him. He made me who I am. If I have intelligence, it is because He gave it to me. If there is love in me, it is because of Him. If I do any good, it is from Him.

In the same thought path, *you* are "fearfully and wonderfully made," a unique creation of God, just waiting to blossom (Psalm 139:14). We are all a work in progress. When we give ourselves up to Him and His guidance, His building of His work in our lives, we can have nothing but good come from it. It is not a perfect life, but is a growth spiritually to become more like Him.

Our ultimate goal is to become like Christ. To become more like Him, we need to know Him. To know Him, we need to spend time with Him, like you would any developing relationship. Spending time, talking, and learning about each other, sharing activities—these are things which increase intimacy.

Share your deepest thoughts and desires with Him. He already knows them, but for you to share willingly and openly is a step of trust. If you need healing, He can help you heal. He may use others in your life as catalysts, but He is the Great Physician. He did not give up that work when He went to heaven to sit at the right hand of the Father.

He can make beauty from ashes (Isaiah 61:3). Actually, He wants to do this for you, and He will—if you allow it. As you begin to allow Him to work in and through you, He will display His might and power.

Your job then is to share it with others. Bless others by sharing what the Lord has done in your life. What a joy to brighten another person's world! To give them hope about what He can do in their life.

In my job as a nurse practitioner, I provide care for a variety of people, from a variety of backgrounds, with various degrees of illness. These people need someone who cares about them. They need sunshine in their lives. Life is complex, sometimes not at all easy, often quite challenging. I cannot fix these folks. I cannot heal them. I cannot go home with them and help. I can be a loving, caring person as God works through me. I can pray for them, listen to them, offer them comfort. Only God can give true comfort. There is so much work to be done. People, indeed, do need the Lord.

Christian folks who are going through hard times struggle, too. It is not that they do not have problems or do not hurt. They do. They have much trouble, deep sorrows, illnesses and grief.

The difference in my Christian clients is that they have a hope. Their hope is in the Lord. As we get older, we know that heaven awaits us. We long for relief from the stresses of this life, from the pains we feel. Heaven is our eternal reward. But that doesn't mean we want to go today! No, truth be known, most of us enjoy being alive. We have tremendous struggles, but we still like life.

There are some who are distressed to the point that they do not want to live. They see no meaning in life. They can find no reason to get up in the morning. Love these people as you cross paths with them. They need relationship. They need God's unconditional love. They need to understand that there is a purpose and a plan to their life. We need to share God with them.

What about Christians who are so frustrated with life that they wonder why God has allowed it to be the way it is? My friend recently lost an aunt. Her uncle committed suicide within two weeks of his wife's death. This couple had one child, who now finds herself alone, orphaned if you will, at the age of about 60. During this time, my friend's husband has been diagnosed with cancer and is undergoing chemotherapy. There are constant changes in her workplace. Her plate is full. Her life is hard. She cries out to the Lord. She trusts Him, but she knows His will may not be what she desires.

What about these kinds of situations? This is not an uncommon story. I see it all the time. But I see God at work in the lives of these Christians. I see the strengthening of relationships and the growth in families. I see folks turning to God who have not given Him a thought in the past.

So it can be with each of us. As we "get real" with God, being honest and open with Him, diligently seeking His will for each day of our lives, He will show more of Himself to us. He will become more real to us. We will grow and will make a difference in the lives of those around us.

Show me your ways, Lord, teach me your paths.
Psalm 25:4 NIV

Chapter 12:
Move Ahead

Where do we go from here? Is surrender an option for you? It truly is in the surrender that we find our freedom in Christ. So—decision, action? Are you ready to move ahead? Are you ready to take that next step?

Step One: If you do not have a quiet time established, do that first. Choose a place where you can be comfortable and focused. Bring any resources you need or want. You may start with just your Bible, or your Bible and a devotional. You may want to use music... worship or praise music to get your mind set on God. There are no demands or expectations on this time. There is no right or wrong way to do it. This is your time to "be still and know that [He] is God (Psalm 46:1)." If you find this difficult, do not give up. Be persistent. Satan wants you to be sidetracked in your pursuit of the Father.

Try journaling in your quiet time. Listen to what the Lord has said. Writing it down helps with the connection. Writing it down helps you remember. It helps you be somewhat accountable. It also gives you a spiritual marker, a resource, and a way to see His work in your life.

A journal is a great way to sort things out. Putting it down on paper seems to make it seem clearer. It is a great way to remind yourself where you have been and what He has done. It can be simple or it can be complex. Some folks use journals to record prayers and the answers.

My own journaling has been sporadic until this year. I took a class at a local church which incorporated journaling. It was such a wonderful experience that I have continued it. Some days are two or three lines. Some days are two or three pages. I found that writing the scripture in my journal seemed to bring it home to me more. It seemed to stick in my brain to be used during the day. The Lord has been faithful to help me recall what I needed when I needed it.

In addition to your own quiet time and devotionals, you should sit under good Biblical teaching. If you do not have a church, find one where you can learn and grow. If you have a church, don't just listen to the sermons. Take notes. Think about them. Talk about them. Explore them a bit more.

If you still want more, still hunger for more, there are several excellent pastors whose sermons are available online. Andy Stanley, Charles Stanley, Chuck Swindoll, and David Jeremiah are just a few (and obviously some of my favorites). They often have Podcasts available or devotionals which are accessible online or with your smartphone.

The YouVersion Bible app is free and an excellent resource with the Bible available in multiple translations. They also have various devotionals and reading plans available. This is a resource you can have with you on your phone. As much as we text today, surely we can use our phones to help us grow spiritually.

Christian books are plentiful and good sources. However, you must weigh what is being taught, whether in books or sermons format, against what the Bible says. We trust that the Bible is the holy, inspired written word of God, and as such, serves as our "plumb line" against which we are to compare the teaching we hear.

Another good option is Christian music. Staying tuned in to God throughout the day helps us in our walk. It helps us keep our mind where it should be. It reminds me to be grateful.

The lyrics to the song that was on my mind when I woke this morning were "your love never fails, it never gives up, never runs out on me." (Jesus Culture, "One Thing Remains") This song is about God's unfailing, unconditional love. It was a reminder to me of His love and His blessing on my efforts. He often uses music to remind me of Himself and of my worth to Him. I praise Him for His faithfulness.

Music is my "go-to." It speaks to my soul. Be cautious about the music you choose to listen to. Make the lyrics stand the test of the Bible before you make it part of your regular diet. Some music does not honor God.

Another important piece of your walk as a Christian is scripture. The words of God written on the pages of the Bible bring life to a dying soul. They are like water to the thirsty. They speak His truth to us and dissipate the lies of the evil one. This is why it is so important to know it, repeat it, and apply it. It is our primary defense—the sword of the Spirit.

When I was a child, I had to memorize scripture. I was going to be in a Bible Drill! We had it at our church, and then moved to the associational level. I had to recite not just verses, but passages of scripture. What a chore! I was nine or ten years old. There were four of us doing this. Our teacher helped us. We even had some weekend nights at her house to work on it. We had so much fun, but it was grueling work, and nerve-wracking at the drills.

Hey, I made it! I survived. Not only that, but the Lord continues to bring those passages back to me when I most need them. I often cannot quote the reference, but I remember the gist of them. Those scriptures have helped me through some very dark times in my life.

I cannot begin to tell you how grateful I have been for the effort my teacher put into that little group of children. Her effort changed my life.

God's word does not return void. He said so in the book of Isaiah. So when God's word goes out, His purpose will be served.

Praise God for His word! Thank you, Lord, for sharing it with us! We are grateful. Help us to utilize it, to incorporate it into our lives, to see how it brings change for the good in us.

If you do not know scripture, or have trouble memorizing, try writing a verse that has meaning to you and carrying it with you. Maybe post it on your refrigerator or your bathroom mirror so you can constantly see it. Think about it through the day. See how it applies to your life. Ask God to reveal it to you—what He wants you to know about it, how He wants you to apply it. Thank Him for His words. As He speaks to you, follow his word. Follow His leadership. He will not steer you wrong. You cannot go wrong with God.

One of the things I have done at home is to incorporate scripture into the décor. (Not that there is much décor, but hey, I have some pictures on the walls...) I have bought these items as I have felt led to. I determined that the Old Testament commandment to post the law on the doorposts could translate into pictures on my walls. These are a great reminder.

The first one I posted is over the door opening to my kitchen: "As for me and my house, we will serve the Lord (Joshua 24:15)." I hope it reminds everyone in my household what our purpose is. Another favorite that my friend Mary gave me is "Be still and know that I am God (Psalm 46:10)."

That verse takes on new meaning when you think about a daily quiet time. That is time to be still with God, and acknowledge who He is. When we recognize Him for who He is, how can we not be with Him? He has requested your presence in that verse, and He has told you what to do. Be still.

He says "Be still, and know that I am God. I will be exalted among the nations, I will be exalted in the earth."
Psalm 46:10 NIV

Chapter 13:
Learn from the Best

I enjoy a peace that I cannot explain which comes from the Lord. It is a joyfulness for the small things. For breath and life, birds and trees, blues skies and clouds. These emotions are welcome to me. I crave them. I long for them, and I can have them if I am faithful to my time with the Creator.

The disciples called Jesus "Master." That term was more accurately translated Teacher. He was an expert on what He taught. The disciples were not his slaves. They were His pupils and His friends.

What did Jesus teach them? He taught them what the Father's will for them was. He taught them life principles. He modeled sacrificial living with appropriate self-care. Jesus gave and gave and gave... Then He pulled away to be refreshed and restored. He modeled for us how to live a life that is pleasing to the Father. His goal was to do the Father's will. If we are to be like Jesus, we too must do the Father's will.

But how can you know the Father's will unless you know the Father? And how can you know the Father? Through time with Him and study of the word. Jesus told us all we need to know. He said, "No man comes to the Father but by me (John 14:6)." He is the way. He will guide us to our destination, and He will see to it that we arrive safely.

Let's take time to learn from the best teacher ever: Jesus. Study the scripture. Follow His example. Model your walk with the Father on His walk... Be His disciple, not just His admirer.

> *"The words I say to you I do not speak on my own authority. Rather, it is the Father, living in me, who is doing His work."*
> *John 14:10b NIV*

Chapter 14:
Words

What if you feel you have no purpose? What if you cannot see a reason for your life? What if you don't think you make a difference at all? I have been at all those spots on my journey. I can only guide you back to the word of God for inspiration and assurance. He knows the plans He has for you (Jer. 29:11). He put you together in your mother's womb. He knows your getting up and your lying down (Psalm 139).

He has a reason for your existence. He has you here to draw others to Him. You are not just window dressing in the kingdom of God. You play a vital role, but you may not understand it until we are with Him in glory. The words you speak can build up or tear down, encourage or discourage (James 3). You choose your words. You choose life or death.

The words you say to yourself are just as important. Your words to yourself can help you be what you need to be, or they can crush your spirit. Bless yourself in your own self-talk. If you cannot come up with something yourself, speak the truth of God back to yourself. You "are fearfully and wonderfully made" (Psalm 139:14). He meant those words when He commissioned their writing, and He still means them today. There are enough messages in our world to tear us down. Don't listen to those lies. Listen to the God of the universe, who you can trust…

If Satan can paralyze you or cause you to be ineffective because of self-doubt or just lack of concern, then he wins. If he wins this skirmish (we know the battle is already won), he effectively causes you to miss out on the blessings of the Lord. And nothing is better than God's blessing. Nothing feels better than being in complete obedience to Him—daily. Daily walking with the Lord brings that peace and joy we seek.

Many people search for peace and joy in things other than God. Some search for it in relationships, alcohol, drugs, sex, even the busyness we mentioned earlier, but none of these things brings peace or joy. You may feel a temporary pleasure, but that cannot begin to compare to the lasting joy in His presence.

So be careful with the words you choose, the words you use. Claim God's blessing on your life. Walk in obedience to Him. Live out your God-given, God-ordained purpose.

The words of the reckless pierce like swords, but the tongue of the wise brings healing.
Proverbs 12:18 NIV

Chapter 15:
Peace

Are you looking for peace? Have you looked to Jesus? You won't find it on the evening news. Or the morning or noon editions, for that matter. You will only find sadness, chaos and hurt. Yes occasionally they do a positive human interest story, but most of what you see or read is bad news. Many times it is gruesome, because we tend to gravitate to the sensationalized ugliness we see in our world. If we did a newscast with just good news, no one would watch it. There would not be enough excitement for our taste.

The world is a scary place sometimes. Yet mankind has not changed. Ecclesiastes tells us there is nothing new under the sun. I have found that to be true. There are alterations of old things, but our sinful nature has remained unchanged. We are, after all, human. We are rebellious at the core of our being. That is why we fight so hard against God, and against rule. That rebellion has never left our hearts.

Although the world is frightening, we cannot be afraid. He will guard and protect us. What about those who die because of the evil of others? I do not know. I just know that God is sovereign above all and that His purpose will be accomplished.

When my daughter was two years old, there was a story in the news of two boys in England who kidnapped and murdered a two year old little boy. They were children themselves... I lived in fear for my daughter's safety even though this atrocity was committed a continent away.

When she was five years old, Jon-Benet Ramsey was found brutally murdered in her own home. My daughter and I had just had Glamour Shots done for fun. People were remarking to me that she looked so much like Jon-Benet! That was tough on a young mother who already feared for her daughter's safety.

The world can be ugly. My poor child was restricted because of something that happened thousands of miles away—because of my fear and my view of the world. Perhaps she hung on to my anxiety, even though I tried to hide it from her. Fast forward eleven years later to another daughter, born to an older mother, a mother with more life experience and spiritual growth. Instead of living excessively fearfully, I encourage this second child to get out and explore the world. Different time, different mother. I have learned to trust the Lord more. I have learned to avoid the news!

I try to focus on things that matter to us as a family, and the things of God. I am trying to live today, and not be controlled by anxieties and fears about things I have no control over. What are we told? 95% of the things you worry about will never happen…

What does the Bible say? "Be anxious for nothing, but in all things, with prayer, supplication and thanksgiving, let your requests be known unto God (Philippians 4:6)." The Old Testament scriptures tell us that we are sheltered under His wings, that He holds us by His right hand, that He hides us in the cleft of the rock.

Just think! Those passages speak about the God of the universe and His care for you!

Whether you choose to accept it as truth does not make it any less true. Truth stands alone.

What is truth? Webster's dictionary (online) defines it as "the real facts about something; the things that are true." Jesus said, "I am...the Truth... (John 14:6) " Jesus stands alone. He is Truth, regardless of your agreement or disagreement. Regardless of who says what... It cannot be changed. It does not need to be changed, but many people try. They try to discredit, erase or disqualify Jesus. Their efforts are inconsequential in changing the truth. The truth sets people free. Jesus sets people free. No two ways about it. What are you waiting for? Your freedom awaits you. And with that freedom, He gives you His peace ...

Peace I leave with you; my peace I give you. I do not give to you as the world gives. Do not let you hearts be troubled, and do not be afraid."
John 14:27 NIV

Chapter 16:
Take a Closer Look

Excuses, excuses. What are yours today? My excuses were I'm too busy. I'm capable of taking care of myself. I have too much on my plate to add a single thing. Some people say He is not real, that it's all a lie. He was a good man but nothing more. Our excuses don't matter a hill of beans. Truth stands. It will not be changed.

Look at your excuse critically. What is it really saying to you? Is it saying that you just don't want to make the effort? That you don't need Him? That He can't help you? Look at it and see what God has to say about it.

What is your schedule like? Does it ultimately honor Him? Or does it just keep you busy? Does it keep you busy so you don't have time to face Him? Is there something that you are ashamed of, and because of that you want to keep your distance from God?

Busy keeps you distant alright. I can tell you all about that. You can be busy doing a lot of good things but not be doing what He wants you to do. And that is what you need to do—only what He wants, in His strength. Don't receive glory for His work.

So back to your schedule—look at it critically. How much time do you have in your day? How do you fill it? Are there things you need to stop doing so you can start doing others? Pray about it. Ask God to guide you, then let Him. Don't ask if you will not let Him…

Think of times when you might incorporate some "God time" into your schedule, even if it is just ten minutes. Think of ways to bring Him into your daily life, like music CDs or podcasts. Favorite pastors may offer internet viewing which will inspire and challenge.

But maybe you don't want challenge. Maybe you like life just the way it is. So be it. But you, and your family, will miss a great blessing by not staying tuned in to God.

I am not asking you to stop all activities that are not church related. I am asking you to see if there are some that you need to eliminate so you can "accommodate" a visit with God. That didn't sound nice, did it? You should look at all activities. Again, you can be busy doing good things, but that may not be what is best. Just look, and pray about it. Then act on it.

Teach us to number our days, that we may gain a heart of wisdom.
Psalm 90:12 NIV

Chapter 17:
Grow, and Be Healthy

What are you doing to promote your own spiritual growth? Do you just show up at church on Sunday morning? Maybe you go to Sunday School or Bible study? Are you applying what you learn, or just nodding your head in agreement if it is a good point? Have you grown spiritually? What is God doing in your life? How is He using you? Who is touching your life? Whose life are you impacting?

Goodness, those are a lot of questions. I need to sit down by myself and think them through again. We should periodically look at these questions and see where we are.

We don't just get saved to decorate the world with our presence. We are here to make a difference. What a difference we can make!

Look at the influence and work of the Christians during the birth of our country, and in its early years. Where could we be with more Christian men and women in the offices of our land today?

Even if you do not hold office as a politician, you are a leader. You lead by default much of the time. The kids watch you. If you call yourself a Christian, you will be observed by many, and people can be very critical of Christians. It behooves us to be on our best behavior, basically so we do not insult or disgrace God our heavenly Father.

Several years ago, I would have said you should behave so you do not make your church look bad. While that is important, that is not the overriding concern. It is really about God. It is all about Him. We know that He is the reason for everything.

Your spiritual health is of prime importance. Just like you take care of yourself physically (at least I hope you do), you need to take care of yourself spiritually. You need a regular check-up. If you were a car, you would get a tune-up. (We call that revival—or at least we used to.) You would get an oil change. Maybe that would be repentance—out with the old oil, in with the fresh oil and maybe a new filter as well.

The principles apply. If you buy a house, you know it requires regular maintenance. Your spiritual life needs routine maintenance also. There are so many illustrations of the importance of staying on top of things spiritually. Preventative maintenance is key but it takes some effort.

And let us consider how we may spur one another on toward love and good deeds, not giving up meeting together, as some are in the habit of doing, but encouraging one another—and all the more as you see the Day approaching.
Hebrews 10:24-25 NIV

Chapter 18:
Set the Stage

You cannot really separate yourself into parts like we try. Your spiritual health is intertwined with all of you and with the world. Your environment plays a role in the health of your spirit. Chaos will beget chaos. Peaceful environments beget peace.

Think of your environment. What do you surround yourself with? How is your home structured? Does it support your quest for spiritual health? Or does it distract you? Some people say they thrive on chaos. I wonder if this is because their spirit is unsettled. I am not judging anyone. I only know about my experience. Simple, non-chaos is what I desire. I am a work in progress, as we all are.

But there is much we can control… We can control our lighting, sound, color and texture. We choose those things in our homes. We may not be able to choose much about our work environment, but if we can take a mental picture or impression of our peaceful spot with us, take mini-vacations in our minds when we feel disrupted, it will do much to bring that peaceful feeling we seek.

Music is a key to mood. If you have fast energetic music, you will likely feel more energetic. If you choose calming melodies, you will feel more calm—most of the time.

There are times when things in life are so chaotic that it seems nothing will help. Maybe that is when you need to cry out to God, to use your voice and share with Him. If life is so chaotic that you cannot find peace today, go back into your memory and go to a place where you were peaceful. Experience it again. Do not let yourself get angry or upset that you are not there today, that life is not the way that you want it just this instant. Life is life. It is not always easy, and it is often hard.

But we are here in this moment, and we need to be present in it. What do I mean? I mean you need to experience every moment as fully as possible. Now is what we have.

Yesterday is what we had. Tomorrow is what we hope for.

Live today! Today—Live. Love. Laugh. Enjoy life. Sing. Praise God. Pray. In the midst of the chaos of life, find your peace in the shelter of the Lord. He loves you. He wants to be close to you, and only He can give you the peace your desire.

Only let us live up to what we have already attained!

Philippians 3:16 NIV

Chapter 19:
Boundaries, not Walls

Sometimes there are people in your life who give you an edge of chaos. These people are in your life for a reason. God has placed them there. Try to find out what He wants you to do, how He wants you to relate to them. It could be in a supportive role. It could be as a prayer partner. It could be that you work side by side with them. Whatever the situation, try to see yourself as a separate person. Do not let their chaos create chaos for you. You cannot live their lives. You cannot make their decisions. You can only love them.

If it is your child who brings chaos to your life, remember that you are their guide. As small children, you can set rules and enforce limits. With older kids, it is more challenging. The challenge is greater still with the adult child who is still your child but is no longer a child. Each of us has to find our way, and with God's guidance and your constant prayer, your child will as well.

Never stop praying for your child. Never stop loving your child. "Love bears all things (1Corinthians 13:7)" does not mean you have to put up with abusive or disrespectful behavior. It means that the love continues…

How you show that love should be decided by our heavenly Father, not by the people in your environment. Each child is different, and there is no cookie cutter approach. Just love them. And in all things, model for them what the Christian life should look like.

Do not try to make their decisions for them. Be open to the fact that your child is not you, and that God has a special work for them, just as He does for you.

Pray for God to continue to work in their heart. Pray for guidance and direction. Pray for God to place people in their path who will lead them to a deeper knowledge of Him.

Engage your faithful friends who know the Lord and who you can trust to pray for your child as well. The Lord is faithful. He will answer your prayer, but ultimately it is your child's decision.

Praise be to God, who has not rejected my prayer or withheld His love from me.
Psalm 66:20 NIV

Chapter 20:
Priorities

What are your priorities? This morning I read the scripture where Jesus said you cannot serve two masters. So is it God or money? This clearly spoke to me in a decision I have to make about my life situation. Hey, the money would be helpful, but the chaos this particular change would bring to my life may ruin it for all of us, because when I am unsettled, it pours into my family's lives as well. Besides, did not the apostle Paul tell us that God will supply all our needs (Philippians 4:19)? I have found this to be true in my life.

When my oldest was in middle school, she wanted to dance. She needed to dance. We needed to incorporate physical activity into her life, and she was not a sports kind of girl. She had danced as a small child, but the studio we loved had closed.

At this time in our lives, as often seems the case, I could not see how we could accomplish this. So I prayed about it. I had my friends pray. I knew in my heart that this was what she needed. I told God that I knew this was what had to be done, what he was directing me to do, but that I did not know where the money would come from. We had bills, mortgage, the usual stuff. My daughter was my main concern. I told Him that I would be obedient to His prompting. He would have to provide.

And provide He did! He met the need. I never missed a payment to the studio. I was able to pay my bills. Our work situations did not change. You may think, "You really changed your lifestyle." Dance is not inexpensive. We did not and do not live extravagantly. We did not adjust. There really was not anything we could change. We did not stop tithing…

But God was faithful… I could not tell you how. No extra deposits in our accounts. No overtime. No changes. But the money was there. Why do I think this happened? Because it was what God wanted and I was obedient.

My stories could continue about God's faithfulness but you might get tired of reading. I can assure you that He has met every need I have had when I have been faithful to be obedient to Him.

So where are your priorities? What is your desire? Do you find yourself placing things and money ahead of God? You may not do it intentionally, but it is easy to slide into that mode unaware. Do you surround yourself, in your inner circle, with people who seek God or people who seek possessions? Are you always comparing what you have or do not have to what someone else has or does not have? Do you feel proud when you know you have more or better?

If so, you need to think about where God is on your priority list. He desires to be Number One. If you are not there, ask Him about it. Ask Him to change your heart to be what He wants. He wants us to be more like Christ. So ask Him to give you the mind of Christ.

Do you think this will happen all at once? Like God will wave a magic wand and suddenly everything is different? Well, I guess it could, but my experience has been one of gradual transformation. "Be ye not conformed to this world, but be ye transformed..." (Romans 12:2) We are called to walk like Christ, but we are not Christ. We cannot expect perfection. It is a daily walk, a daily choice, a daily surrender to His will.

And quite honestly, every day is not the best. But just keep trying. Keep putting one foot in front of the other. On the days when I am at my darkest, when I see no end in sight, when I want to throw in the towel and run away, when I think I cannot go on—I cry out to God, and I just keep putting one foot in front of the other. One step at a time is all I need to do. It is all I can do. It is all the strength I have.

But remember to walk in His strength. When you try to do things on your own, you will grow weary and want to give up. But when you walk in His strength, you are energized. You are capable because He provides. He gifts you. He works all things for good if you are His...even your mistakes.

The Lord is my strength and my shield; my heart trusts in Him, and He helps me.
Psalm 28:7a NIV

Chapter 21:
Prepare

So do you think that if God asks you to do something, you only have to say yes and you will accomplish it effortlessly? In many instances, you have to take steps to prepare for whatever He has called you to do. If you decide to plant a garden, you will have to prepare the soil, purchase the tools, seed and fertilizer, and you will have to tend that garden as it grows.

So it is with the things God calls you to do. Some things are easy and do not require preparation, like buying the meal for the person behind you in the drive-thru. Someone did that for me once. What a lovely surprise and a kindness that I needed to experience that day! Or speaking a kind word when God prompts you. That does not take preparation, just listening and response.

Other things do require you to prepare... like leading a class, starting a different job, or getting a degree so you can be a missionary. I have no way of knowing the variety of things God calls you to do. But you do. It is your decision how to respond. Listen carefully. Discern that it is God speaking, and choose wisely. Then prepare yourself.

Study to show thyself approved unto God, a workman that needeth not be ashamed, rightly dividing the word of truth.
2 Timothy 2:15 KJV

Chapter 22:
Seeking Support

How do you engage others in your spiritual journey? Let your closest friends and family know what you are trying to do. Ask them to pray for you. Understand that sometimes people will look at you like you have three heads. Some will try to discourage you and some will be antagonistic. Some may be angry or offended. Some may think you are being uppity.

Remember that when you are growing, you are a threat to the evil one, and he will do all he can to discourage you. He will challenge you by asking how do you know this is what God wants? This is where your journaling comes in handy. As you look back on your life and circumstances, you can see God's hand moving you in the direction. And if you do not see that? Pray. Pray until you have clarity and peace.

A changed you may mean a changed home life. Sometimes a spouse may be threatened by your enthusiasm or plan. Remind your spouse that your love them. That is why you married them. Remind them of your commitment to them. As you become more spiritually in tune with God and His will for your life, your attitudes will change, and you will find the peace you search for.

This change is gradual. Start with small steps like daily devotionals and scripture reading with journaling. Engage supportive Christian friends. You may want to join a small group. If your church does not have one, consider starting one, or attending a small group at another church. God has many resources out there to help you get to where He wants you to go.

If you are not currently in a Bible believing church, or your church is unhealthy, prayerfully consider where you should be. Ask God to direct you to a church where you can grow and be nurtured spiritually.

Brothers and sisters, pray for us.
1 Thessalonians 5:25 NIV

Chapter 23:
The Journey of a Lifetime

You are the only one who can take care of you. You have that responsibility. If you are not where you want to be spiritually, do not blame your church. If you follow God's leadership, He will put you exactly where you need to be in this season of your life.

Again, you may encounter resistance, even from your longtime Christian friends. If you find this to be the case, try not to be angry with them. Pray that God will do a work in their lives so they can experience a closer walk with the Lord as well.

Remember, this is the journey of a lifetime, and it takes a lifetime… What an adventure to live life with God and in His will! He has a lot in store for you, for us, for the church. Hang on and get ready for a fun ride! He won't let you down. He will never leave you or forsake you.

Cling to Him in the good, the bad, and the ugly times. Make your choice. Be your best. Life apart from Him is nothing. He is the very reason for your existence.

He loves you unconditionally. He desires your company. He wants to make a difference in your life. He wants *you* to make a difference in the lives of others.

Why wait? What's stopping you? Let it go, and go with God. We are in this together, united as the Christian church universal. We are here to serve, teach and disciple.

God's call is on your life. It may not be to become the next Beth Moore or Billy Graham, but He has a work for you to do. And, my friend, you will not find satisfaction until you do it.

The things of this world will pass away, but the things of the spirit, the things of God, will last forever. If you want to make a difference of eternal proportions, here's your chance. There is no time like the present to start to work on the eternal…

God bless each of you as you journey with Him!

The one who calls you is faithful, and He will do it.

1 Thessalonians 5:24 NIV

Epilogue

Well, I finally finished my book! What a privilege to have written it, to be able to share with you the words from my heart. God is faithful and has provided me all that I have needed to complete this project.

The basic manuscript was completed during my writing seminar, but the culmination took longer for a variety of reasons. All in due season, the timing is not mine, but His.

I experienced a bout of depression after completing the book... I was on the verge of publication when I lost my focus, my drive and my interest. After having written what I felt was such a positive book, to experience this depression made me feel like an imposter and a fake ... For months, I could not bring myself to complete it. I wrestled with the picture I had painted and my current reality. I questioned how I could possibly experience this depression when I had been so deeply involved with God, when I had clearly felt His presence and his guidance.

I struggled with this paradox in my life. I had known the task set before me was one He had given me, had allowed me to complete, and had led me through. Yet here I was, bogged down in a quagmire of my emotional state, having lost my enthusiasm for completing the assignment.

I struggled in this time. I prayed during this time asking for answers, dealing with the questions and the emotions.

One day I was speaking with my friend Mary Jo, who often helps me sort through my thoughts and feelings. We were leaving work, and I was burdened. I shared with her my dilemma. She was the first one to whom I had confided my struggles. Interestingly, without my prompting, she responded by voicing to me the conclusion to which I had arrived: my book was not finished. I needed to share this experience with my readers.

God is so good. He confirmed his work in me, and His word to me, through Mary Jo in that moment. My hope was renewed. My purpose was reestablished. I began to try to sort through what to share and how to share it.

This took another year or more to come to fruition. When my frustration would resurface, I would be reminded that this work is not about me. It is His work through me, and it is His timing that I need to seek.

My depression waned, and I was back to normal. But I did not complete the book. The depression returned again the following summer, and at that point I sought help from my personal physician, Dr. Chris Sawyer, a trusted man who is also a believer and follower of Jesus. He helped me overcome the symptoms. My enthusiasm for life returned.

Why am I sharing this with you? I share it for two primary reasons.

One, I want you to know that depression is a reality even among believers who are living in close relationship with Jesus. It is not due to a lack of spirituality or lack of faith or lack of trust. It does not mean you are weak or a hypocrite in your faith. Certainly we desire spiritual health as well as physical health. Our emotional health is influenced by these things, but depression is not the fault of the person who experiences it. It happens, and it is a vicious cycle of hopelessness and helplessness which can occur to varying degrees. Unless you have experienced depression, it will be hard for you to understand this.

Secondly, God is at work in your life, even when you do not see it or feel it. King David expressed his depressive symptoms in the Psalms. He cried out to the Lord for relief, for assurance, for rescue. If David, a man after God's own heart, experienced depression, why would we be surprised when we do?

God is faithful. He will use our experiences to grow us to be more like Christ and to prepare us to minister to others who need our help and our understanding. I have seen it in my own life. You will see it in yours as well, if you allow Him to work through you.

Depression may wax and wane, or it may be chronic. All I know is that I am His, and one day when I meet the Lord after this life, I will be whole forever more.

Sharing this experience makes me feel vulnerable, as does sharing the words in my book. But if you benefit from these words, if you grow in your relationship with Jesus, if you find hope, then my vulnerability is worth it. My prayer for you today is best said in the following scripture:

> The Lord bless you and keep you; the Lord make his face shine on you and be gracious to you; the Lord turn his face toward you and give you peace.
> Numbers 6:24-26 NIV

Best regards,
Anna Moore

This book is written with the assumption that you have a personal relationship with Jesus. If you do not have a personal relationship with him, I urge you to consider it today. He is the way, the truth and the life. It is only through Him that we can have a restored relationship with God. The following scriptures will lead you on the path to Jesus. Read them aloud. Think about yourself in relation to the words in these verses. If you would like to accept God's free gift of salvation, it is yours for the taking. All you have to do is receive it.

> For all have sinned and fall short of the glory of God.
> Romans 3:23 NIV

> For the wages of sin is death, but the gift of God is eternal life in Christ Jesus our Lord.
> Romans 6:23 NIV

> Jesus replied, "Very truly I tell you, no one can see the kingdom of God unless they are born again."
> John 3:3 NIV

Jesus answered, "I am the way and the truth and the life. No one comes to the Father except through me."

John 14:6 NIV

If you declare with your mouth, "Jesus is Lord," and believe in your heart that God raised him from the dead, you will be saved. For it is with your heart that you believe and are justified, and it is with your mouth that you profess your faith and are saved. As Scripture says, "Anyone who believes in him will never be put to shame."

Romans 10:9-11 NIV

And he died for all, that those who live should no longer live for themselves but for him who died for them and was raised again.

2 Corinthians 5:15 NIV

Here I am! I stand at the door and knock. If anyone hears my voice and opens the door, I will come in and eat with that person, and they with me.

Revelation 3:20 NIV

Coming to a right relationship with God is as simple as ABC:

Admit you are a sinner and have made mistakes.

Believe that Jesus died to save you.

Confess him as Lord of your life.

A simple prayer to express this to God might say some thing like "Lord, I know that I am a sinner in need of a savior. I believe that you came to earth as a baby, lived a perfect life without sin, died on the cross for my sin, and rose again in victory over death. I ask your forgiveness and accept the free gift you offer me today. I want you to be Lord of my life."

If you have chosen to become a follower of Jesus today, I welcome you to our family. I encourage you to find a Bible believing church where you can grow and be discipled. I pray that God would bless you now and in the days ahead.

About the Author

Ann grew up in rural East Tennessee, the seventh child in a family of eight. She was raised in church from the time she was a toddler. She accepted Christ as a child, and was always active in church. However, the activity of church did not meet her deepest heart need. It was as adult, a wife and a parent that she began to be truly discipled and to understand what it meant to have a personal, intimate relationship with God. Today, her desire is to share with others in hopes that they will come to the understanding of this amazing opportunity to be in relationship with the God of the Universe.

About the Book

This book is written as an invitation to the reader to explore a deeper relationship with God. Questions are posed, thoughts are shared, and steps to furthering the relationship are explored. The book reflects the author's experiences and lessons she has learned as she has journeyed along her life path. It explores not only the "why", but the "how to" of a deeper walk with God, and challenges the reader to seek Him in a more deliberate manner.

www.ingramcontent.com/pod-product-compliance
Lightning Source LLC
Chambersburg PA
CBHW031647040426
42453CB00006B/240

9781627470902